THE GREAT UNTAMED

POEMS TO SHARE

Compiled by Catherine Baker

Illustrated by Yuzhen Cai, Bryony Fripp and Alexis Snell

OXFORD

UNIVERSITY PRESS

OXFORD
UNIVERSITY PRESS

Great Clarendon Street, Oxford, OX2 6DP, United Kingdom

Oxford University Press is a department of the University of Oxford. It furthers the University's objective of excellence in research, scholarship, and education by publishing worldwide. Oxford is a registered trade mark of Oxford University Press in the UK and in certain other countries

British Library Cataloguing in Publication Data

Data available

ISBN: 978-1-382-04089-1

10 9 8 7 6 5 4 3 2 1

The manufacturing process conforms to the environmental regulations of the country of origin.

Printed in China by Golden Cup

Acknowledgements

Series Editor: James Clements

Compiled by Catherine Baker

Illustrated by Yuzhen Cai, Bryony Fripp and Alexis Snell

Every effort has been made to contact copyright holders of material reproduced in this book. Any omissions will be rectified in subsequent printings if notice is given to the publisher.

'Enormouse' by Sally Roberts published in The Dirigible Balloon. Reproduced by permission of Sally Roberts.

'Friends' by Karl Nova published by Caboodle Books on 27th October 2017. Reproduced by permission of Caboodle Books.

'Yeti on the Settee' by Joshua Siegal published by Bloomsbury on 19th August 2021. Reproduced by permission of Bloomsbury.

'Cuttlefish' by Pamela Jones published by The Dirigible Balloon in 2023. Reproduced by permission of Pamela Jones.

'Stars? Dust? Us?' by Inua Ellams published by The Emma Press on 29th September 2016. Reproduced by permission of Inua Ellams.

'The Moon Speaks' by James Carter published by Otter Barry Books in 2012. Reproduced by permission of Otter Barry Books.

'Howl' by Zaro Weil published in *I Hear the Trees* by Hachette in 2023. Reproduced by permission of Hachette.

'Hesitant' by Pallab Chaudhury published in Poem Hunter on 7th January 2023. Reproduced by permission of Pallab Chaudhury.

'Dream Dust' by Langston Hughes published in *The Collected Works of Langston Hughes* in 2002. Reproduced by permission of Harold Ober Associates, Inc.

'I Will Sing' by Matt Goodfellow from *Bright Burst of Colour* published by Bloomsbury in 2020. Reproduced by permission of Bloomsbury.

'Swallowed' by Shauna Darling Robertson in *Wonder: The Natural History Museum Poetry Book* by Macmillan in 2021. Reproduced by permission of Shauna Darling Robertson.

'Carpark' by Catherine Baker, first published in *Readerful The Great Untamed: Poems to Share*, 2024.

MIX
Paper | Supporting responsible forestry
FSC www.fsc.org
FSC™ C110497

Contents

Enormouse

You do not see when I am there,
My footsteps make no sound.
I slip softly by you, unaware,
And my home is underground.

I squeeze through places you can't see
And nobody remembers me,

For my ears are small
My tail is thin
My whiskers are minute.

My fur is dull
My paws are weak
And my squeak is almost mute.

But do not doubt me
Don't ignore me
And please don't call me cute.

For I have something you can't see,
Something strong inside of me.
You may think I'm just a dormouse
But you can trust me: I'm enormouse!

Sally Roberts

Cuttlefish

The cuttlefish seizes
The chance when it pleases
To show off its prizes,
Its colourful guises.
When danger arises
The cuttlefish chooses
Some clever disguises
And brilliant ruses.

The cuttlefish uses
A plan it devises,
A plan that confuses
And often bemuses.
A plan that comprises
Its inky surprises
The cuttlefish oozes
(sometimes hypnotises).

The predator loses
And off the prey breezes.
The danger defuses
And nervousness eases
The colour arises
The cuttlefish snoozes.
The end.

Pamela Jones

Swallowed

When humans didn't know any better,
all the swallows flew to the moon each autumn
and returned to planet earth in spring.

And since the moon has no stoneflies, sawflies,
mayflies, damselflies, the swallows adapted, got fat
on mooncrumbs and double cream.

And as there wasn't much of an atmosphere,
no air up there for sound to travel in, the swallows fell
quite silent for a full six months

or so they told us each April, by then bursting
to spill a backlog of chatter. Hundreds of years
it took us. Hundreds – to catch up, cotton on, *capeesh*

that the other side of the world exists
and that's where the birds go to winter.
Nowadays they send us postcards from Maputo,

Kruger, Bulawayo, Drakensberg, The Cape.
Or they WhatsApp us snaps of a sunset, desert, beach
sometimes adding in (LOL) a splash of cream.

Shauna Darling Robertson

Yeti on the Settee

There's a yeti
on the settee
as of yet he
won't get off

It seems petty
but he's sweaty
(I regret he
has a cough)

With my threat he
is beset, he
gets upset, he
tries to fight

so I'll let the
sweaty yeti
on my settee
stay the night

Joshua Seigal

The Moon Speaks!

I, *the moon*
would *like it known – I*
never *follow people home. I*
simply do *not have the time. And*
neither do *I ever shine. For what you*
often see at *night is me reflecting solar*
light. And *I'm not cheese! No, none of*
these: no mozzarellas, *cheddars, bries, all*
you'll find *here – if you please – are my*
dusty, empty *seas. And cows do not*
jump over *me. Now that is simply*
lunacy! *You used to come and*
visit me. *Oh do return,*
I'm lonely, *see.*

James Carter

Stars? Dust? Us?

The clever ones say
zillions of days, billions of weeks,
millions of years ago,

    stars   e x p l o d e d

  into   f i e r y

              clumps

                           of   dust

  that cooled

         down to sea,

                   stone, soil,

  to human beings,
and I am made of stars.

Everything we are is everything they were.
Everything they were is everything we are.

So were stars made of me?
　　　of denim jeans,

　　　　　　　　　dark chocolate,

　　　　　　pressed flowers,

　HOT sauce,

　　　　　waffles,

football,

　　　　t a d p o l e s

　　　　　　　　and t   m   l e
　　　　　　　　　　u   b   s

millions of years ago,
zillions of days, billions of weeks,
were stars also scared of darkness what do
the clever ones say?

Inua Ellams

Dream Dust

Gather out of star-dust
Earth-dust,
Cloud-dust,
And splinters of hail,
One handful of dream-dust
Not for sale.

Langston Hughes

Hesitant

Having crossed rivers
and lakes, being hesitant
to cross a puddle!

Pallab Chaudhury

I Will Sing

I've spent
a long time
listening

catching words
that slip
from lips
and stick
to my hair
my clothes

my skin

I've collected
each unit
of sound
each feeling

kept them close
for the day
when

I will sing

Matt Goodfellow

Friends

There's nothing like having a friend that understands you
who stands with you when others just can't stand you
In a world of lies a true friend stands true
always on standby to stand up for you
it's great when you click with someone so easily
and it's not forced at all, it doesn't need to be
If life were a song you're both in harmony
You're always laughing with them so heartily
My friends are always in my heart you see
I am part of them and they are part of me
"birds of the same feather flock together"
is what I've heard said I hope we fly forever
and if in the future we part ways
I hope we meet in the sky and bask in sun rays
In my heart is where a true friend stays
because friends touch our hearts
and the fingerprint stays

Karl Nova

Howl

AIEEEEEEE AIEEEEEEE
　　OUEEEEEE OUEEEEE
　　　　OUOUOUOU OUOUOUOU
howl little one
howl
don't hold back
　　flash those polished
　　　　amber eyes of yours
　　　　　　howl the scent of long ago
and
　　if I teach you anything
　　　　know this new-found voice of yours
　　　　　　calls forth the great untamed
so
when you want sun to rise
　　night to ignite its silent sparks
　　　　clear water to swell the river
howl

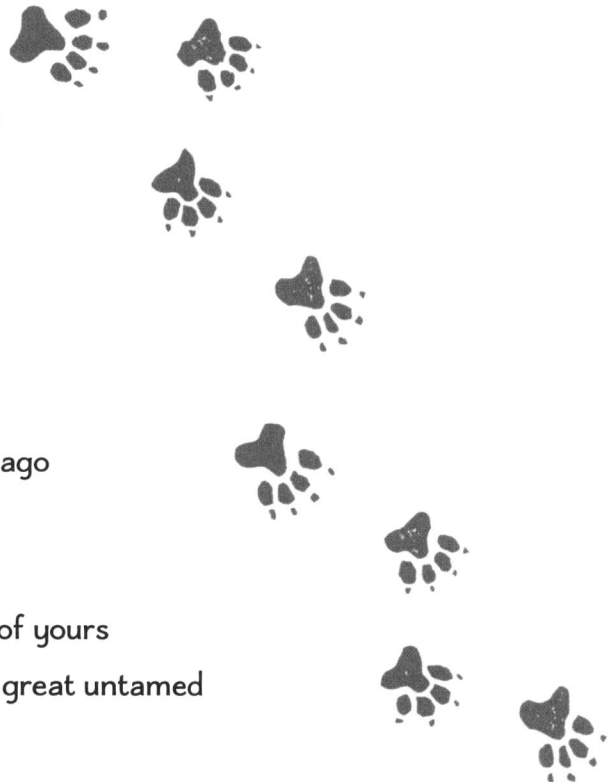

and when you stand
      stiff-legged and tall
          proud ears alert
              teeth sharp-shined
                    confronting your prey

howl
      of course when you must fly
          escaping the bear
              howl fierce
                    for earth to rise up fast
                        to meet your lengthening legs

then howl soft
      when first you meet your
          grey-furred partner
              under a moon-flood of trees
                  on a trail of sweet shadows

and
howl long
      when you smell that blue
          of berries growing darkly wild
              outside your very own den

last thing little cub

     when I am no longer

          hunting beside you

          howl full

               your big wolf heart

               for me

AIEEEEEEE AIEEEEEEE

    OUEEEEEE OUEEEEE

        OUOUOUOU OUOUOUOU

Zaro Weil

Something Told the Wild Geese

Something told the wild geese
It was time to go.
Though the fields lay golden
Something whispered – 'Snow.'

Leaves were green and stirring,
Berries, lustre-glossed,
But beneath warm feathers
Something cautioned – 'Frost'.

All the sagging orchards
Steamed with amber spice,
But each wild breast stiffened
At remembered Ice.

Something told the wild geese
It was time to fly –
Summer sun was on their wings,
Winter in their cry.

Rachel Field

Carpark

Breathing together,
all our patient blunt-nosed cars –
their hot mammal breath
thickening the air a while
and then idling to nothing.

If you turn back now
you'll see distance has changed them,
their wraparound eyes
blank and glossy with sunlight,
their hard insect elytra.*

Abandoned all day,
is it us they're waiting for?
At some distinctive signal
will delicate wings unfold?
Will they all rise together?

Catherine Baker

* Elytra (say: *el-i-truh*) are the hard, shiny wing cases of insects like beetles.

The Eagle

He clasps the crag with crooked hands;
Close to the sun in lonely lands,
Ring'd with the azure world, he stands.

The wrinkled sea beneath him crawls;
He watches from his mountain walls,
And like a thunderbolt he falls.

Alfred, Lord Tennyson

Thunderstorms

My mind has thunderstorms,
  That brood for heavy hours;
Until they rain me words,
  My thoughts are drooping flowers
And sulking, silent birds.

Yet come, dark thunderstorms,
  And brood your heavy hours;
For when you rain me words,
  My thoughts are dancing flowers
And joyful singing birds.

W H Davies